NEW ENLARGED EDITION

Blues & Rag Piano Styles

Arranged for Piano by Bill Irwin

D1601841

Catalog Number 07-2017
ISBN #1-56922-091-3

Produced by John L. Haag

Exclusive Distributor:

CREATIVE CONCEPTS PUBLISHING CORPORATION

2290 Eastman Avenue #110, Ventura, California 93003

Bill Irwin

In 1989, Bill Irwin celebrated his 50th year as a professional keyboardist, educator, lecturer, arranger and author.

He has performed concerts and conducted keyboard workshops throughout the U.S.A., Canada, New Zealand, Australia and Japan.

His music articles have appeared in KEYBOARD, MUSIC JOURNAL, CLAVIER, SHEET MUSIC, KEYBOARDS TODAY and HURDY GURDY.

Bill has recorded two courses of keyboard instruction for the Music Section of the National Library Service, Division of the Blind and Physically Handicapped in the Library of Congress, Washington, D.C. These courses are available free of charge. Blind Institutes and Societies in foreign countries have requested the loan of Bill Irwin's recorded courses for their handicapped members. Some of his study books are in Braille in the Library of Congress.

He is a member of A.S.C.A.P. (American Society of Composers, Authors and Publishers), former President of the Organ and Piano Teachers Association and formerly Editor/Publisher of the national magazine MODERN KEYBOARD REVIEW.

He has lectured to music students at colleges and universities around the country. His study books and arrangements are available in many countries.

In the world of contemporary keyboard music, Mr. Irwin has gained recognition for his efforts in presenting new concepts in arranging, teaching and performance for both students and teachers.

CREATIVE CONCEPTS PUBLISHING CORP. is proud to present this unique collection of standard tunes arranged by Bill Irwin. Truly a "creative concept."

ARRANGER'S NOTES

To Amateur Pianists and Piano Teachers:

This collection of Intermediate Piano Solos is the direct result of the wonderful acceptance of the previous four volumes presently available from Creative Concepts.

As in the other volumes, I emphasize here the use of modern harmonies to lend a modern flavor to the musical standards chosen for your playing pleasure.

The aim is to make the arrangements sound full, harmonically rich and rhythmically interesting with only a moderate demand for playing technique that is well within the reach of the intermediate player.

My arrangements are ideally suited for the pianist with smaller than average hands, as I am only able to reach a ninth interval and arrange the tunes accordingly.

If you have any comments or suggestions, I'd like to hear from you. Write to me c/o Creative Concepts Publishing Corp. If you'd like an answer, please enclose a stamped, self-addressed envelope. Thank you.

Sincerely,

Bill

Alabama Jubilee
by George L. Cobb

Arr. by Bill Irwin

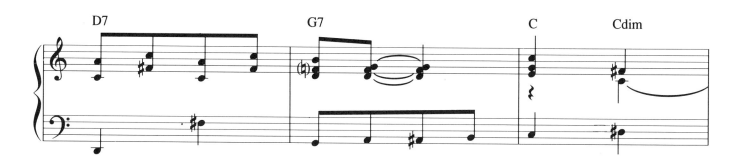

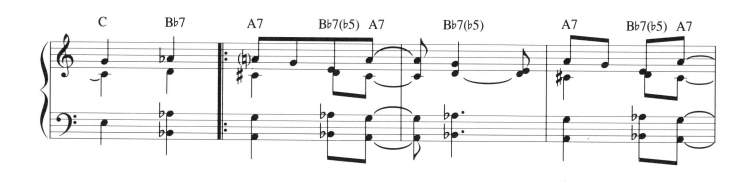

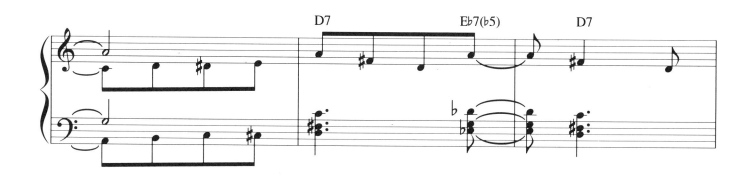

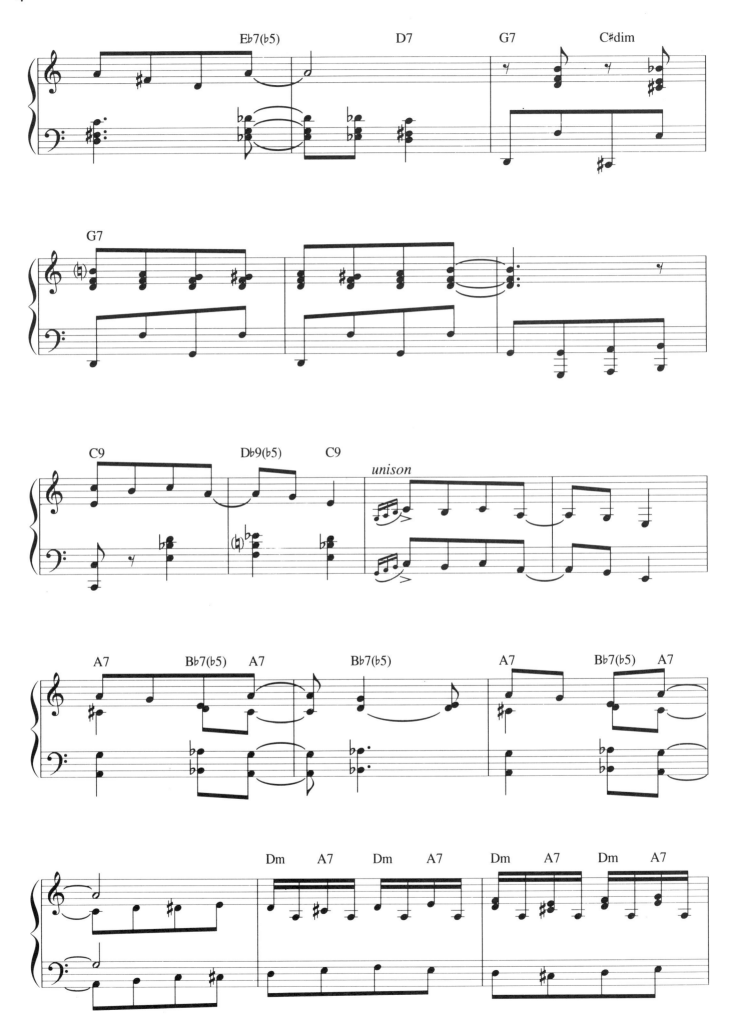

After You've Gone

by Henry Creamer and Turner Layton

Arr. by Bill Irwin

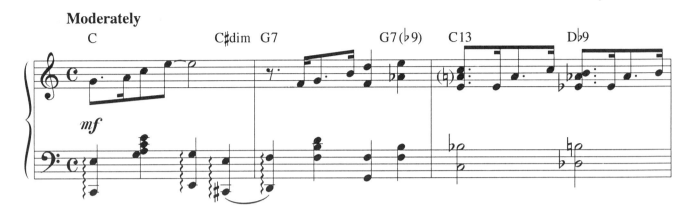

Baby, Won't You Please Come Home

BY CHARLES WARFIELD AND CLARENCE WILLIAMS

Arr. by Bill Irwin

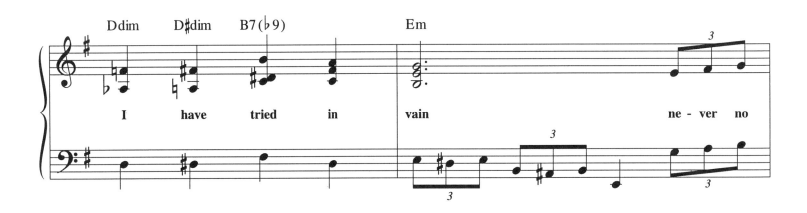

10

Bumble Boogie

BY N. Rimsky-Korsakoff

Arr. by Bill Irwin

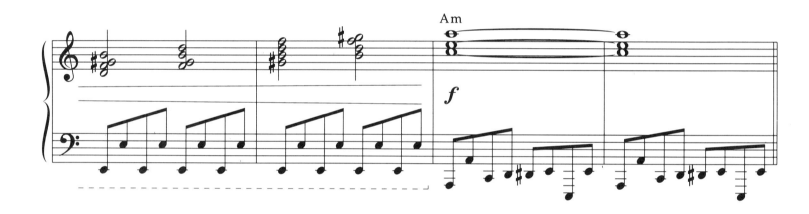

FROM THE MOTION PICTURE "THE BRIDGE ON THE RIVER KWAI"

COLONEL BOGEY MARCH

BY KENNETH J. ALFORD

(F.J. RICKETTS)

Arr. by Bill Irwin

Dill Pickles

BY CHARLES L. JOHNSON

Arr. by Bill Irwin

20

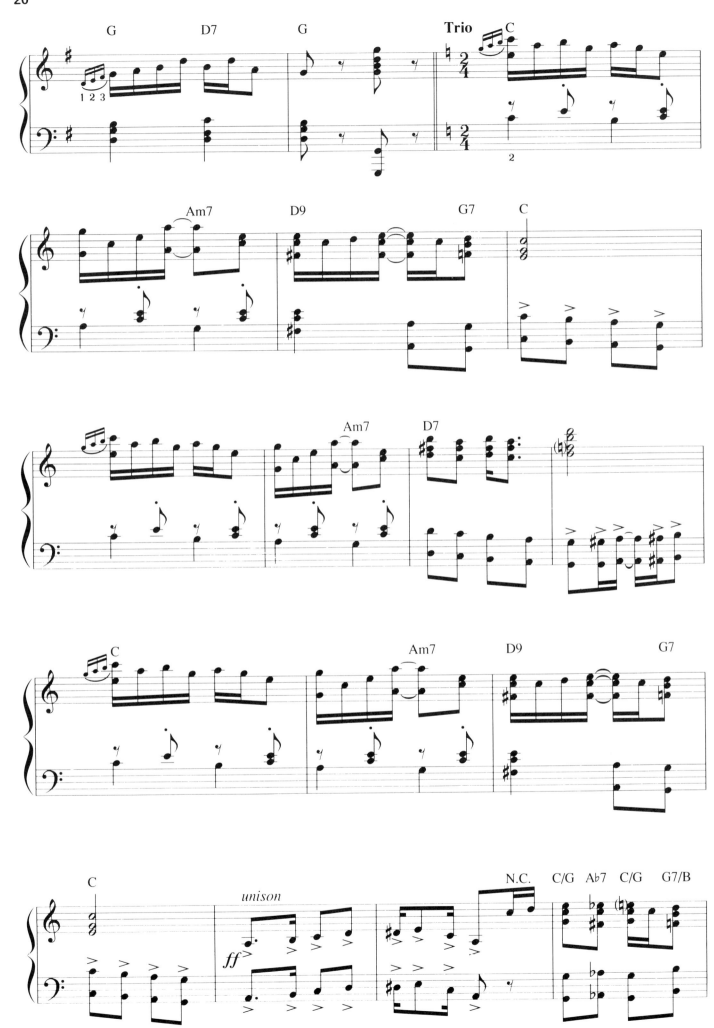

I Ain't Got Nobody

by Spencer Williams

Arr. by Bill Irwin

24

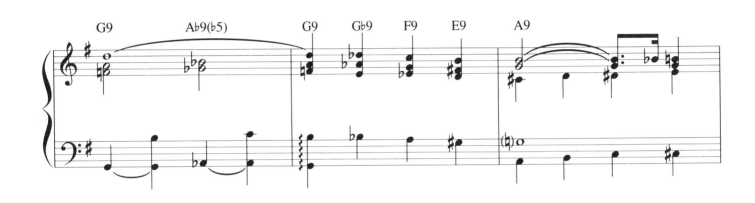

I Love A Piano

BY IRVING BERLIN

Arr. by Bill Irwin

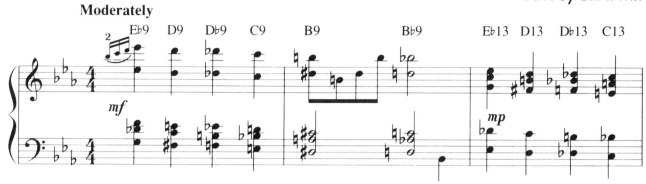

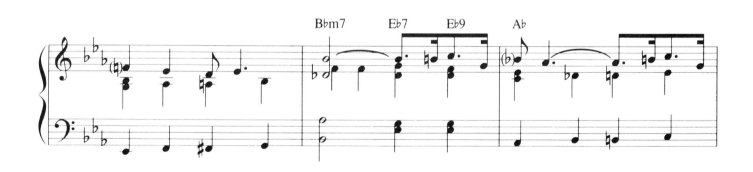

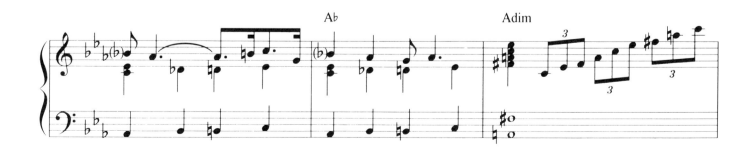

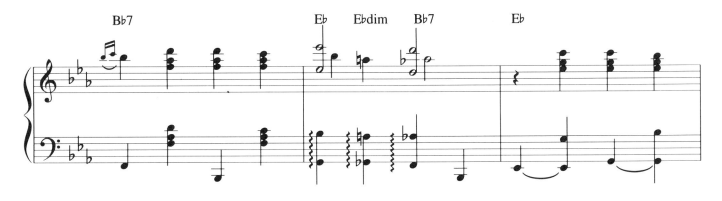

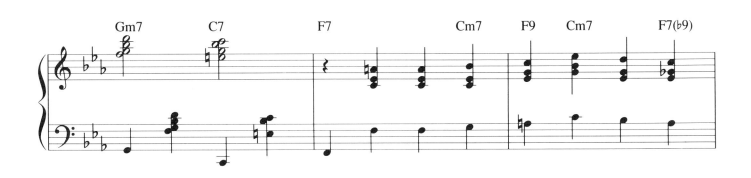

The Jelly Roll Blues

BY JELLY ROLL MORTON

Arr. by Bill Irwin

Johnson Rag
by Guy Hall and Henry Kleinkauf

Arr. by Bill Irwin

Nola (A La Ragtime)

by Felix Arndt

Arr. by Bill Irwin

Moderately (not too fast)

The Memphis Blues

BY W.C. Handy

Arr. by Bill Irwin

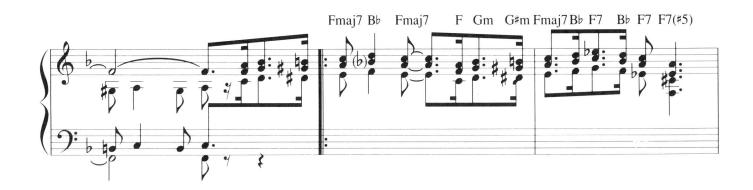

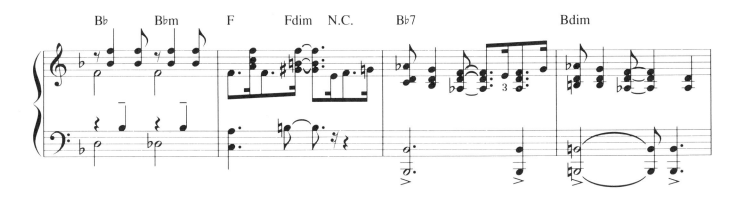

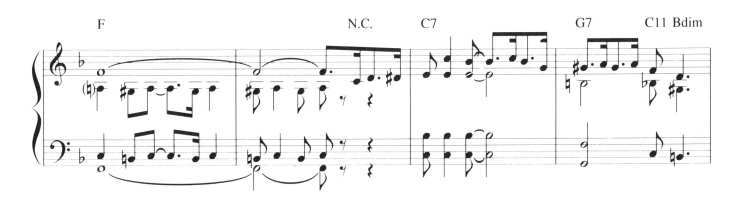

St. Louis Blues

by W.C. Handy

Arr. by Bill Irwin

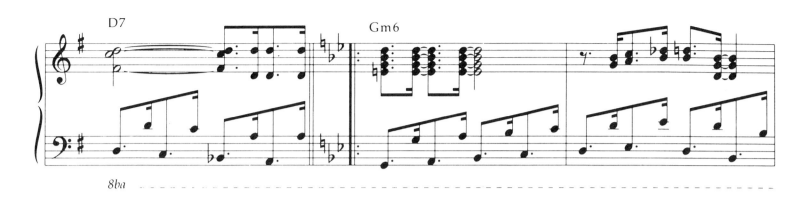

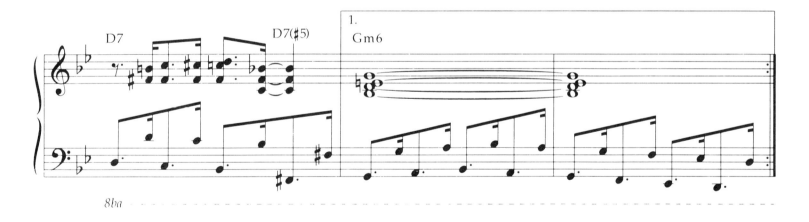

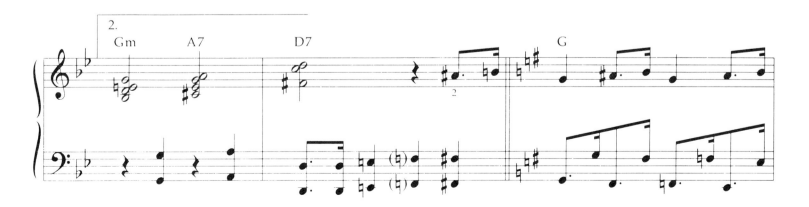

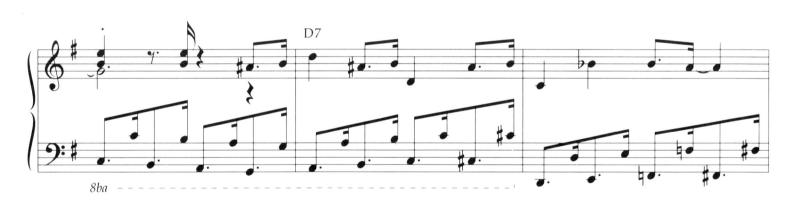

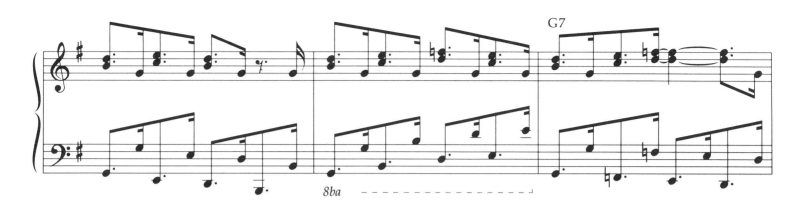

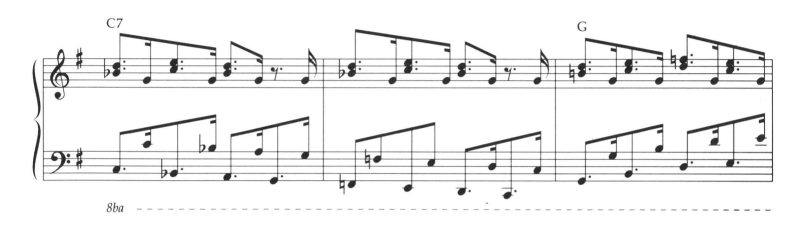

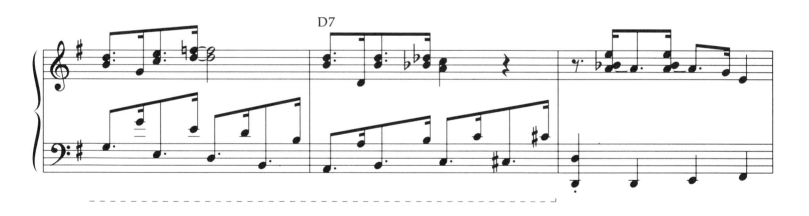

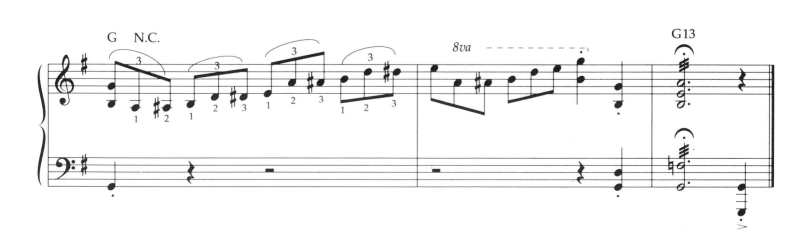

Some Of These Days

BY SHELTON BROOKS

Arr. by Bill Irwin

49

Sugar Blues

by Lucy Fletcher and Clarence Williams

Arr. by Bill Irwin

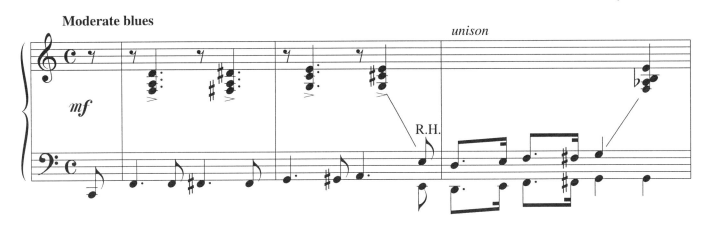

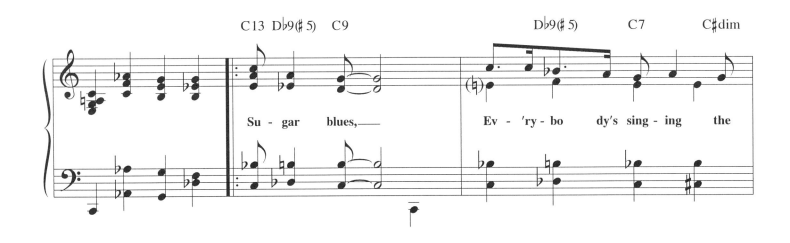

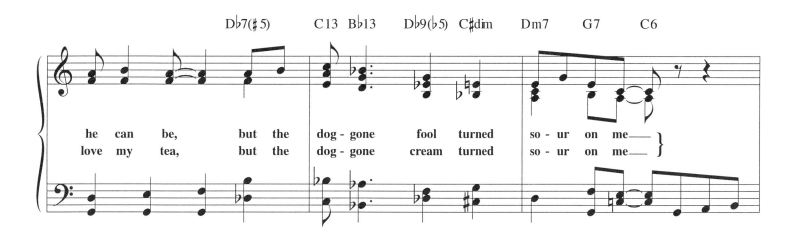

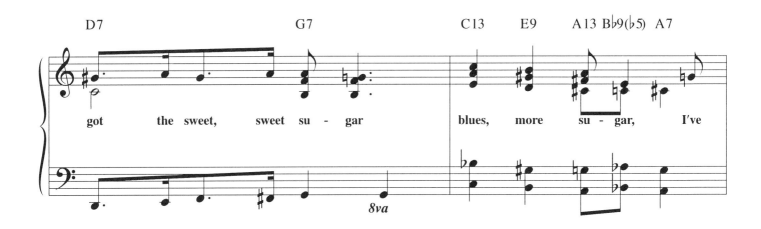

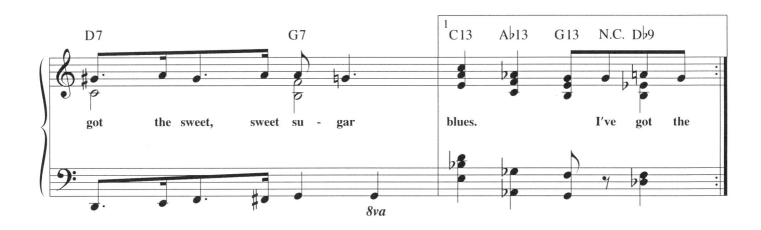

Swanee

BY George Gershwin and Irving Caesar

Arr. by Bill Irwin

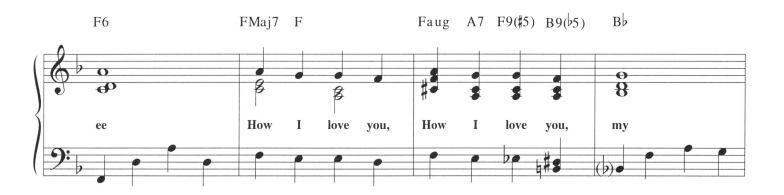

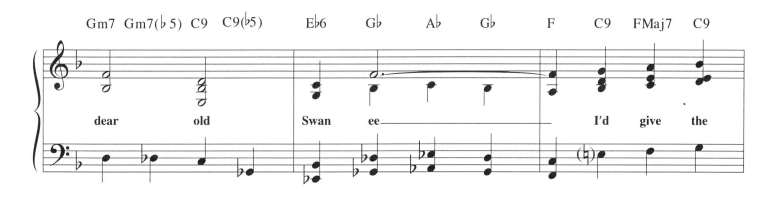

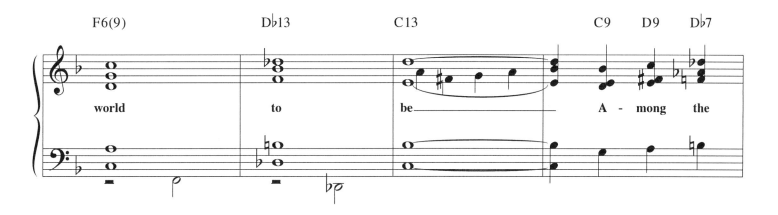

54

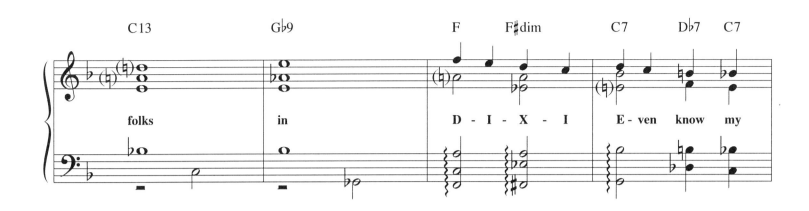

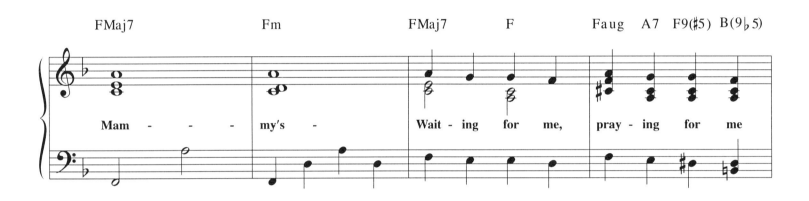

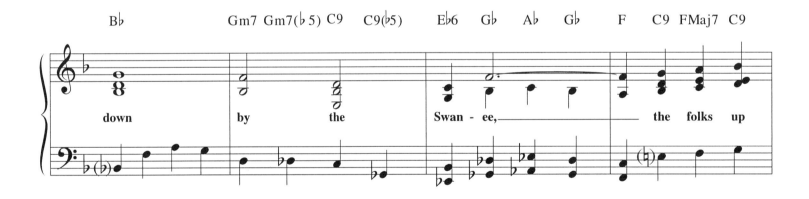

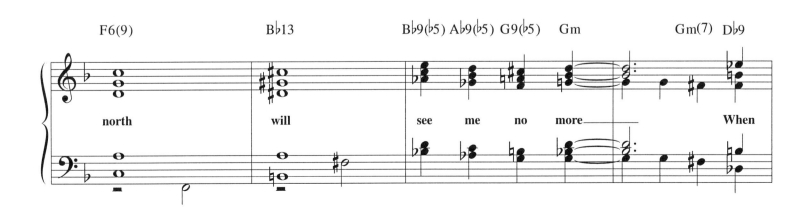

Sugar Cane

BY Scott Joplin

Arr. by Bill Irwin

Moderate Rag Tempo

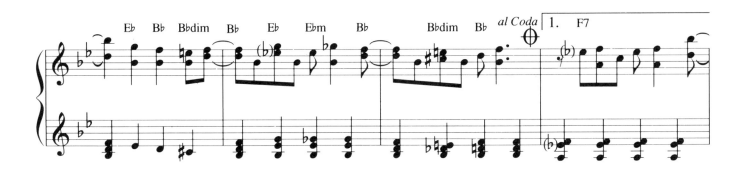

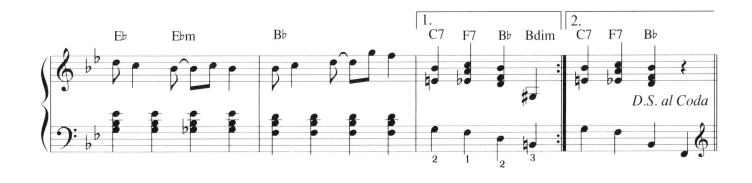

58

Tiger Rag (Hold That Tiger!)

By The Original Dixieland Band

Arr. by Bill Irwin

How fast can you play it?

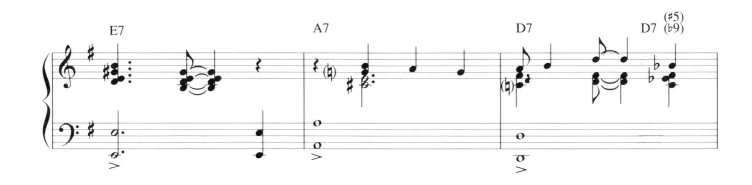

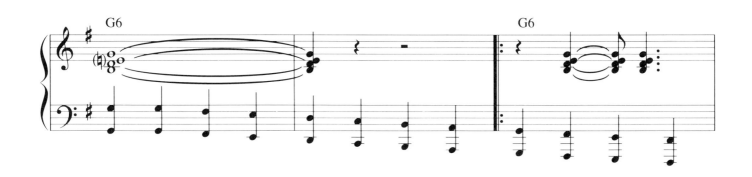

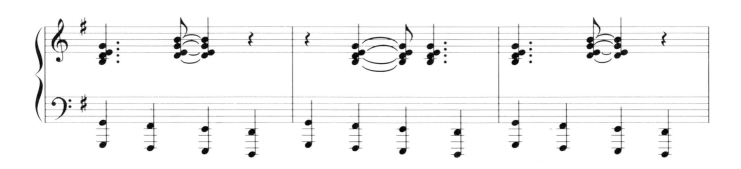

Yellow Dog Blues
by W.C. Handy

Arr. by Bill Irwin

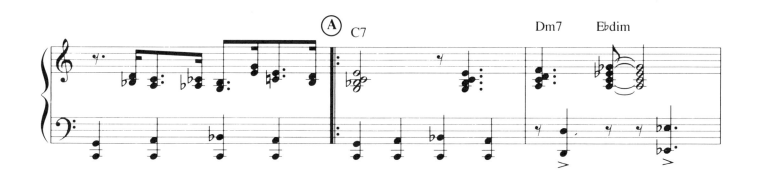

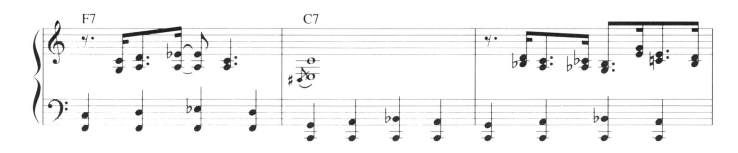

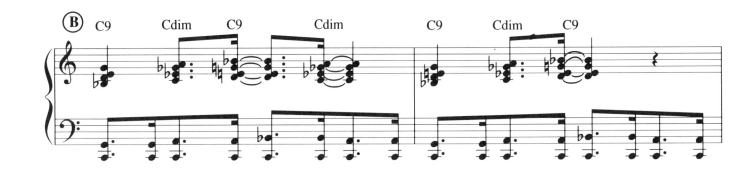

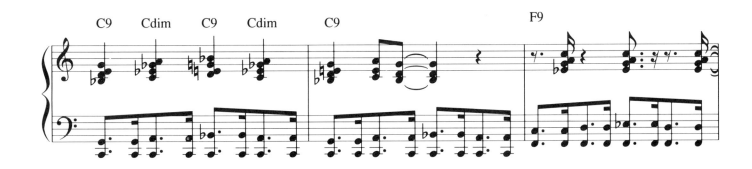

66

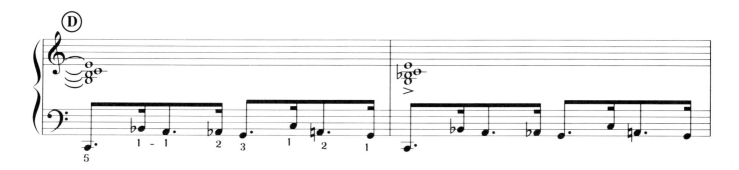

F9   C7

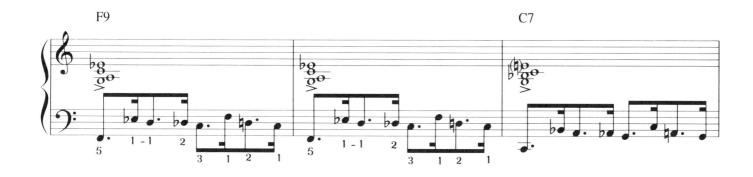

                                                      G7

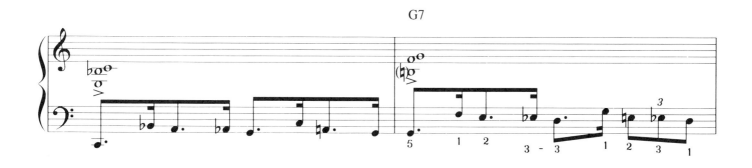

F7   C7

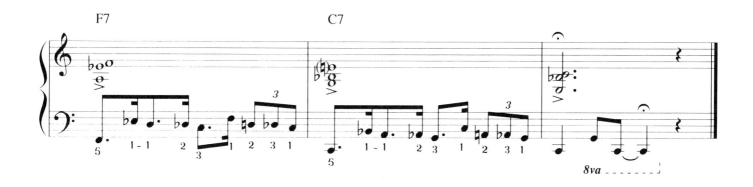

That's A Plenty

by Lew Pollack

Arr. by Bill Irwin

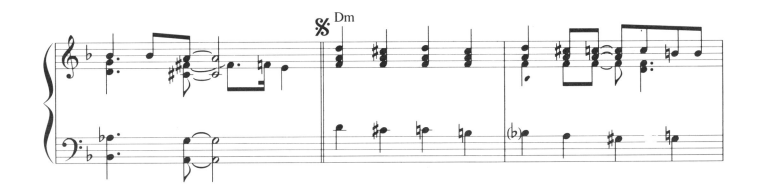

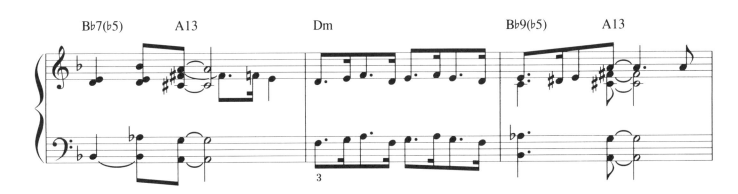

Dm

B♭7(♭5)   A13   B♭7(♭5)   A13   *al Coda* ⊕

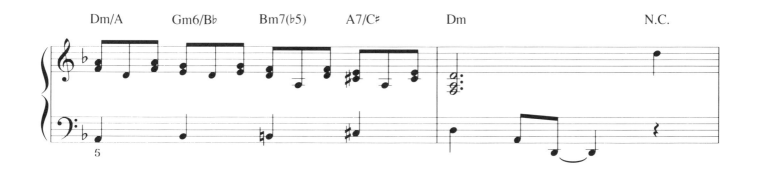

Dm/A   Gm6/B♭   Bm7(♭5)   A7/C♯   Dm   N.C.

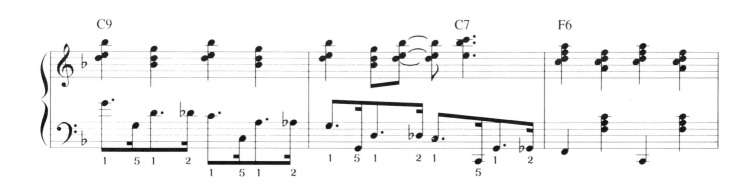

C9   C7   F6

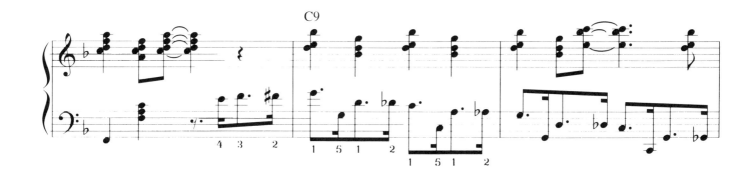

C9

Too Much Mustard

By Cecil Macklin

Arr. by Bill Irwin

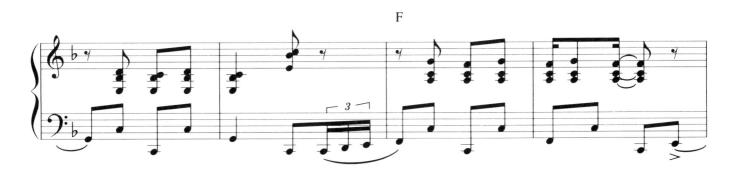

12th Street Rag

BY EUDAY L. BOWMAN

Arr. by Bill Irwin

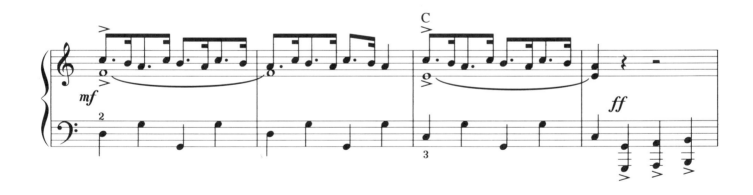